THERE'S A LOT OF NOISE IN SILENCE

Matt and Kim Simpson

Copyright © 2020 by Matt and Kim Simpson
First Edition 2020

All rights reserved.

No part of this publication may be reproduced, stored in a retrieval system or transmitted in any form or by any means without the prior written permission of the authors.

"You should sit in Nature for 20 minutes a day...
Unless you're busy, then you should sit for an hour."
-Zen Saying

"Daddy, stop talking. Listen to the birds."
-Abigail Simpson, Age 2

Once upon... well, not a time,
but an average, typical day.
In a land... well, relatively close really
and not so far away.

The Forest was alive
(and pretty loud for being quiet!).
Time's ignored when the fire roars;
you're captivated by it.

There's a lot of noise in silence,
the birds they know it's true.
And with their songs and friendly calls,
they'll never lie to you.

The embers, they glow bright
as you slowly sneak away.
With wandering thoughts of wonder
to see what you'll learn today.

Like a fox, you quietly leave behind
the tracks that you will make.
Your awareness grows like the water flows
on your way to a Nature break.

You meander off the trail and happily hug a Maple.

Or choose a Pine? Take your time, you only need to wait till...

You find a secret place for you (though the birds know where you've gone!).

To visit over and over and over again, forging long forgotten bonds.

Oh look! You've found **THE** spot that's right for you,
you've got a certain feeling.
It's comfortable, it has a view
and the blue sky for a ceiling.

The great big tree above shadows
both you and their friend;
a grey old rock (for sitting on!)
with laugh lines on its grin.

Unhurriedly, you sit down
and nestle in your spot.
You fuss, adjust, wiggle and jiggle...
then wrestle with your thoughts.

"It's hard to sit still!" you shout up at the clouds,
but they don't seem to mind.
They smile right back, "Shh... not so loud!"
as they gently float on by.

You sit...
 and wait...
  and quiet your mind.
Be calm...
 breathe deep...
  and take your time.

You know, there truly, really, actually **IS** a lot of noise in silence!

(It's an absolute reliance on a natural alliance!)

There's so much emerging all around
when you take the time to notice.
So you make a map to mark it down
and appreciate the slowness.

Each time you visit you seem to find
new things to explore.
New tracks and trails, new thoughts, new tales;
it's never as before.

Or wait... is that new? (Well, maybe to you...)
Or are you more aware?

Is Nature unfolding the
mysteries she's holding
as you start to care?

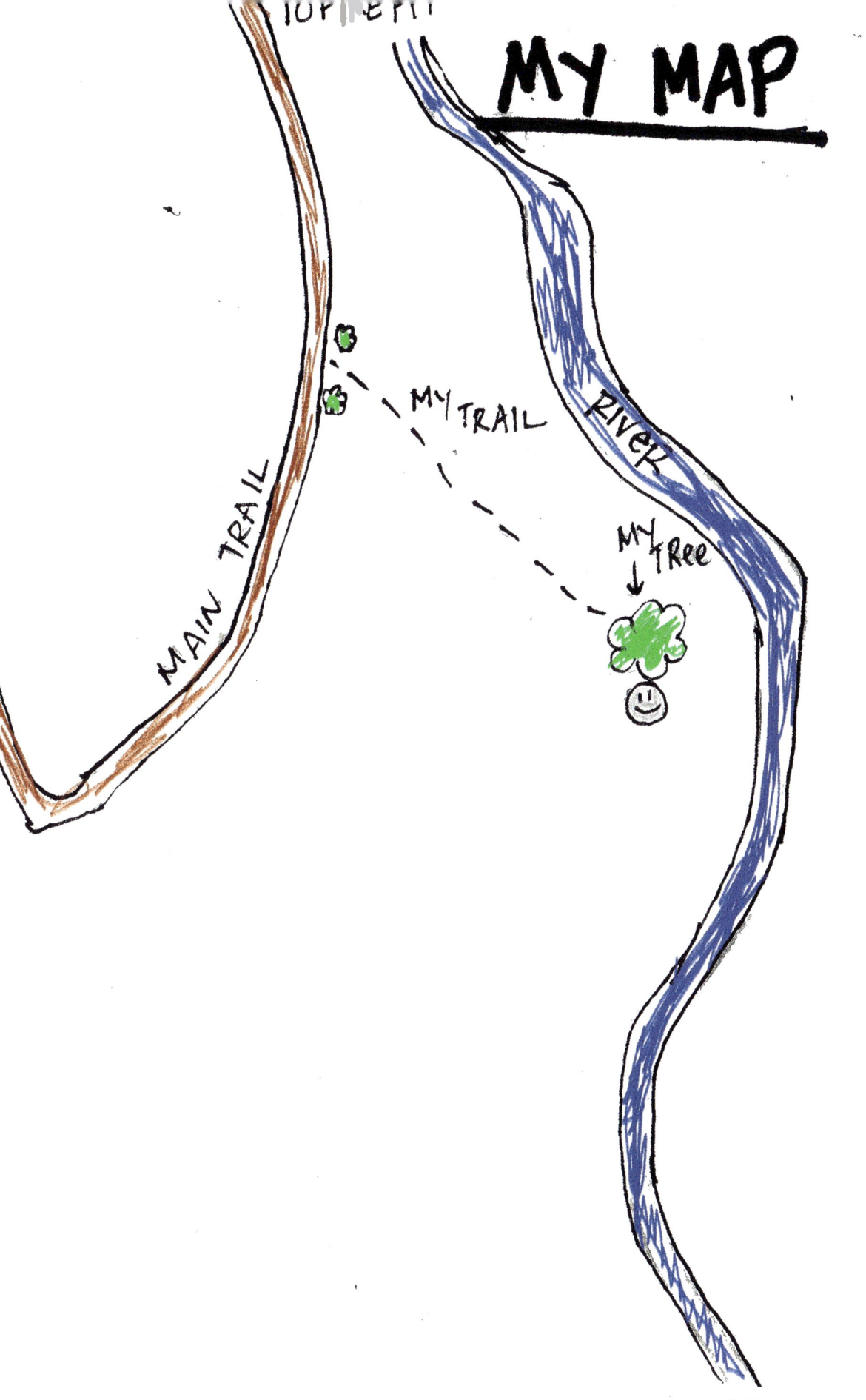

And You Notice:

When the birds appear (and where they live and eat!).

You can also name most critters crawling around beneath your feet.

Throughout the day your Raccoon pal loves to take his nap...

And these important things you know you mark them on your map.

And You Notice:

When your eyes are closed, the heartbeat of your tree.

You hear all the sounds unheard to you when life moves too swiftly.

The water moving underground, the leaves that dance and flap...

You uncover all these wonders (and mark them on your map).

And You Notice:

Each subtle snowflake difference...

...and tree branch squirrel highways.

The friendly tree buds take their stand,
while Juncos shy away.

As Spring arrives more birds do, too,
and Winter does unwrap...

You note these things (and many more!)
on your growing map.

There are Cardinals playing laser tag
and Chipping Sparrows sewing.
Songs surround you everywhere -
the Forest is all knowing.

"Potato Chips!" says Goldfinch.
"Cheeseburger!" cries Chickadee.
As the Eastern Towhee encourages you
to always "Drink Your Tea!"

And with all this talk of food
you look around and roll your sleeves.
Miss Violet isn't feeling blue
and wears her heart upon her leaves.

Her purple flower you devour
to satisfy your belly.
A wholesome snack and when you get back
you can make a wild jelly!

And as you sit you start to learn
you're never quite alone;
with connections stemmed from long ago
you start to feel at home.

Your friends surround you, day by day,
North, West, South and East.

It's solitude,
not loneliness
and makes you
feel at peace.

Well, my friends, that's it for now -
I guess I may have lied...
For if truth be told, it's no normal day
for you to be outside.

So find a quiet place that's loud -
embrace the noisy defiance!
And I'm sure you'll come to know real soon
there's a lot of noise in silence.

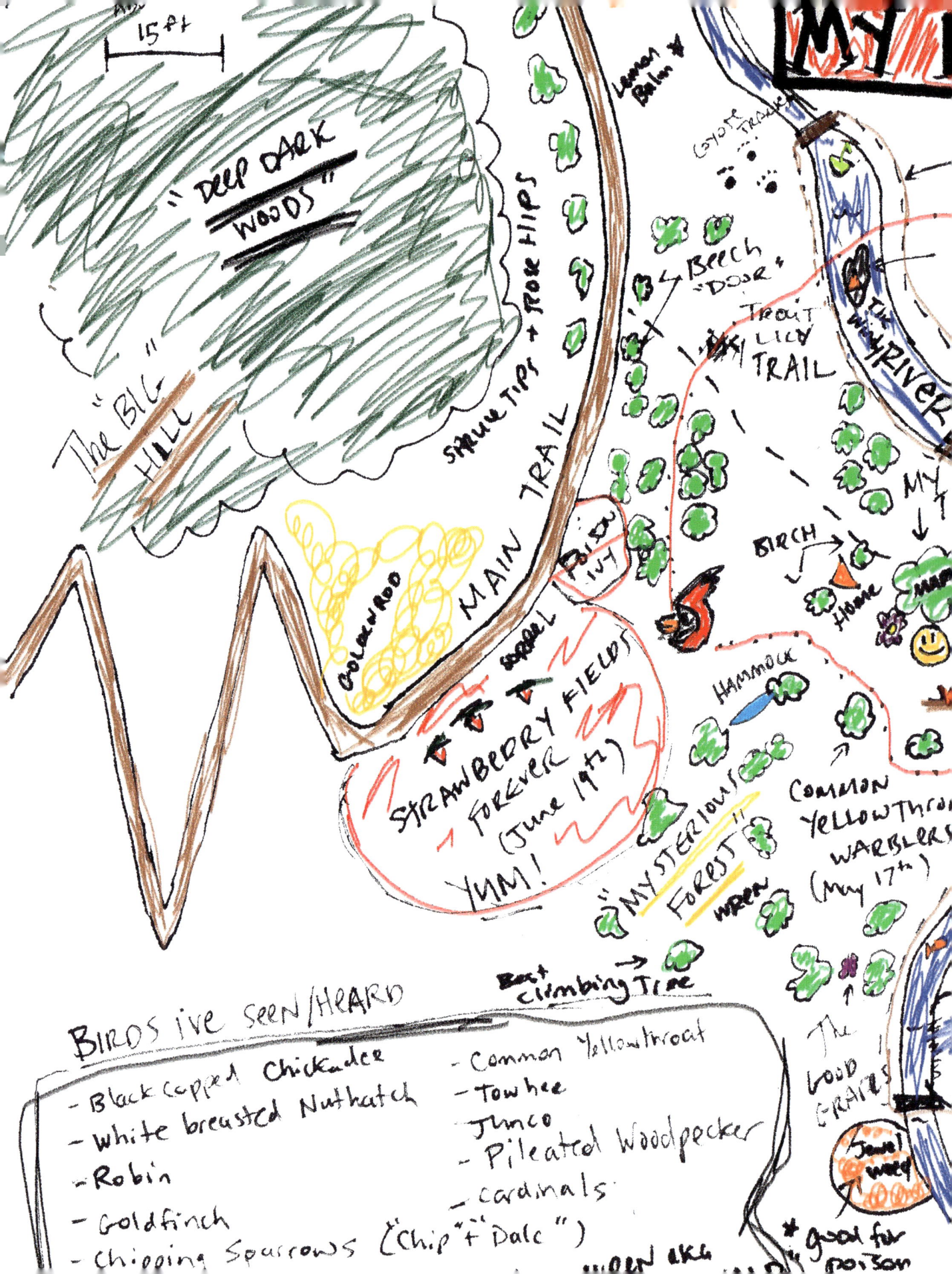

N
Garlic Mustard (invasive)
Loop
(15 min slow walk)
Poison Ivy
Rabbit Hole
(tracks?)
"Maple Forest"
Owl lives here
The ok grapes
Dead Porcupine (Dec 7th)
Leeks
Pileated woodpecker
Little Rapids
Swimming Hole!
little creek
Grassy island
Legend
Black capped chickadee Nest
Fire Pit
Dam (I built)
Violets
Bridge
Sap Buckets
Mini Boat
Main Trail
My Trails
Tree
Shelter
Water
My Rock
Approximate Cardinal Territory
Strawberry
Good Fishing Hole

WILD VIOLET JELLY RECIPE

2 cups of wild Violet flowers

2 ½ cups of boiling water

½ cup of lemon juice (or a freshly squeezed lemon)

1 box of pectin

3 ½ cups of sugar

DIRECTIONS

Collect fresh Violet flowers.

Rinse the flowers and put them into a glass container.

Pour the boiling water over the flowers and cover the jar with a lid.

Allow the flowers to infuse the water for at least 4 hours (preferably overnight).

Pour the Violet water into a pot (through a sieve to separate the flowers).

Squeeze the lemon into the infused water (watch for the colour change!).

Add the box of pectin and mix well.

Stir over high heat until the mixture reaches a heavy boil. Boil for one minute.

Add the sugar all at once. Keep stirring and boil for another minute.

Put it in jars and voila, a wholesome wild snack!

SIDE NOTE: Before you eat ANYTHING from Nature, be 100% sure you know what it is. Check at least 2-3 references or consult with someone you trust who knows about wild edibles. When in doubt, don't eat it!

For our little explorers,
Abigail Ruth and Sadie Lynn Aurora.

ABOUT THE AUTHORS:

Matt and Kim Simpson live in Meaford, ON with their two daughters. They have a passion for empowering folks through meaningful outdoor experiences by nurturing connection with Self, Others and Nature. You can often find them hiking local trails, paddling nearby rivers or simply just listening to the birds. They are the founders, as well as directors and teachers, at Free Spirit Forest and Nature School - a not-for-profit series of Nature Connection Education programs in the Southern Georgian Bay area.

This is their first book!